Green Fingers and Muddy Boots

Ivor Santer

Green Fingers and Muddy Boots

A Year in the Garden for Children and Families

Illustrated by Lucy McCririck

Floris Books

First published in 2009 by Floris Books

British library CIP Data available

ISBN 978-086315-692-2

Printed in Singapore

Contents

Introduction

So you want to be a gardener?

Looking after an area in which you grow flowers, fruit or vegetables is known as 'gardening'. It includes taking care of a patch of ground outside, as well as looking after pot plants in the house and a variety of other plant containers, which give you the opportunity to grow flowers, herbs and even some vegetables and salad crops. Gardening covers all the jobs that are done to care for plants, from planning and planting to weeding, pruning, harvesting and recycling waste materials through the compost heap.

Gardening involves 'doing things', but to be a successful gardener also requires a little basic understanding of how plants grow and what is needed to get the best results through the seasons. You will learn by practice and experience and there will be some failures; occasionally plants will not grow well and some may die. But the positives will outweigh the negatives as you watch the seeds you have planted and the young plants you have nurtured grow into beautiful flowers and tasty fruit and vegetables.

How to use this book

This introduction to basic gardening has been produced for children who want to grow plants and have fun finding out about their local environment. Gardening jobs can be carried out at almost any time of the year. *Green Fingers and Muddy Boots* gives simple, seasonal instructions on how to grow flowers, fruit and vegetables and get the most enjoyment from a range of gardening activities. The programme of activities suggested requires positive work by the young gardener and at times support from a parent or supervising adult. Many children will be capable of working through the activities by themselves. However, the most enjoyment and best results will generally be achieved when the exercises are carried out as a group or family with help from Mum, Dad or a supervising adult. The activity sheets are suitable for group projects at school or with a youth group. At all times the young gardener is encouraged to get help and advice from newspaper and magazine articles, gardening books, the Internet and responsible adults, preferably an enthusiastic gardener.

The activity worksheets listed on p10 are downloadable from the accompanying CD, and can be undertaken even if you don't have access to a conventional garden. There are activities relating to the local environment that involve observing and recording the weather, insects, birds and animals. The broad range of activities correspond with the information provided in the book, and links are given in the relevant chapters. Indications on when to complete each activity are provided in the seasonal guide to gardening at the end of the book.

Gardening activity sheets

Damselfly

Young Gardener Certificate

To encourage young people to start gardening, The Royal Caledonian Horticultural Society (The Caley) has developed a Young Gardener Certificate as a reward for those young people who successfully complete the range of gardening activities suggested in this book. The certificate is of course optional, but gives the young gardener a goal to work towards. There is no set time to start or finish the activities in the Young Gardener Certificate programme. The activities are not intended as an examination or test, but to show that the young person has made an effort to do the exercise to the best of their ability and to have fun doing it! Excellence and perfection come with experience and practice.

On completion of each activity the worksheet must be signed off on the Record of Achievement (activity sheet 35 on the accompanying CD) by a responsible person, who will confirm, in their opinion, that the task has been completed to an acceptable standard.

REGISTRATION

In order to be eligible for the Young Gardener Certificate, you must apply to the Royal Caledonian Horticultural Society, Edinburgh, using activity

Bee

sheet 36, which can be found, along with further information on the Young Gardener Certificate, on the accompanying CD. The Caley will issue a registration number for each certificate. A Young Gardener Certificate will only be awarded if the person/group is registered and the Caley has received a completed Record of Achievement form.

Getting Started

Your garden environment

Every garden has its own particular 'environment' which is influenced by a number of factors:

- The height above sea level (altitude).
- The direction it faces, whether north or south.
- The amount of rain that falls and the drainage conditions will determine whether your garden is wet or dry.
- The amount of sun and shade are determined by surrounding houses, fences, hedges and trees. Many plants will not grow well in shady areas; they need light and space.
- The wind can damage plants and stunt growth, so they will need protection on exposed sites.

These all contribute to your garden environment and determine the types of plants you can grow. When choosing a site to grow plants, particularly vegetables, try to select an area with good, deep, well-drained soil, with plenty of sunlight and no competition from trees, hedges or other large plants growing nearby.

But remember, you don't need a garden to start gardening. Plants can be grown in pots, plastic bags and any type of container that will hold compost or soil.

What a plant needs is:

P — place
L — light
A — air
N — nutrients
T — thirsty (water)

Tools and equipment

You will need a few tools and pieces of equipment in order to start gardening. Garden tools have been designed to help the gardener grow crops and flowers; they make the work easier. Every gardener will need a spade, fork, hoe, hand trowel and fork, and a pair of secateurs to get started. Today, strong materials are used to make garden tools that will last a lifetime, but remember that they can be dangerous if not used correctly. Always work safely and never use damaged or broken tools. Some garden tools, such as the lawn mower and hedge trimmer, are powered by a petrol or electric engine. These tools should not be used by children.

Tools don't have to be brand new or cost a lot of money and you don't have to buy them all at once. Sometimes when people are moving to another area, they will give away their garden tools or sell them at a very reasonable price. Advertisements in the local paper can often be a good, cheap way to find tools. Get in touch with a local gardening club or society; they may be able to get you some tools and offer advice.

Tools and their job

Spade

Used for digging and turning soil. Don't try to lift too much soil in one spadeful; you could hurt your back.

Fork

For digging stony soil, breaking down clods for a finer tilth and shifting compost. Take care when using a fork.

Secateurs

Sharp, clean, scissor-type secateurs are used for pruning and deadheading plants. Take care when using them.

Rake

Used in dry conditions for levelling soil when preparing a seedbed. Do not break down soil clods with the rake — that's the job for a fork. For best results, the soil should be slightly dry. If the soil is cloddy and dry, put your feet together and shuffle along the piece you want to break down, then level with a rake.

Hoe

Use it for slicing through weeds on the surface of the soil and to loosen the ground around bedding plants and shrubs. Keep the blade clean and sharp for efficient operation. There are two types — a flat push hoe and an 'L' shaped pull hoe.

Hand trowel
Used for planting-out, potting-up and all those fiddly jobs that can be difficult with other larger tools.

Hand fork
Used for hand-work when weeding and working around bedding plants or pot plants.

Watering can
Many gardeners use a hosepipe for watering but a can is useful for pots, grow-bags and for giving liquid feed. In dry weather, water regularly.

Garden twine or string
Use it to tie back plants.

Pen knife
A clean, sharp knife is used for taking cuttings. A knife is dangerous; only use it when supervised by an adult. Keep it in the garden shed or tool cupboard.

Plant labels and marker pen
Don't forget to label all newly sown seed trays and pots. You can also use labels to identify seeds and plants in the garden.

Garden brush
For sweeping up leaves and debris — keeping the garden neat and tidy so it looks cared for. Use a hard bristle garden brush.

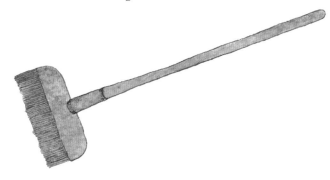

Cloth
A wipe with a clean, dry cloth will ensure that tools will be in good order the next time they are needed.

ACTIVITY SHEET 4 — GARDEN TOOLS

Accidents and first-aid

There are hazards and risks in everything we do, but if you are careful, alert and use common sense, the garden need not be a dangerous place. Of course there is always the possibility of an accident, an insect bite or sting and pathways can become slippery. As a general rule if you keep the garden tidy and you are careful when doing any garden jobs, the chances of an accident will be very small.

Wasp

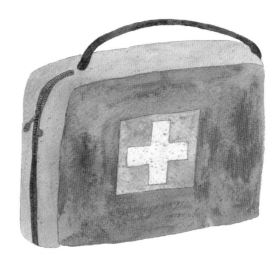

Here are some key things to remember in order to stay safe in the garden:

- Always take care when using garden tools and put them away safely after use. A tidy garden is a safe garden.
- Continuing to work with broken tools will cause accidents.
- Balls and other toys should be put away after play.
- Sweep pathways regularly. Wash green slimy areas with soapy water.
- Never eat any plant, fruit, berry or fungi (mushroom) unless you know exactly what it is and that it is safe to eat.
- Remember that chemicals, fertiliser and garden paint should not be handled by children. Always store them in a safe place.
- Always wash your hands after gardening or handling plants and seeds as some plants, such as nettles, may irritate your skin.
- In case of any accident, make sure you know where to find the first-aid box and plasters for minor cuts.
- In case of an emergency, always have your doctor's telephone number handy, or dial 999.

ACTIVITY SHEET 5 — HAZARDS IN THE GARDEN

Nature's Garden

Trellis

Climate and weather

Climate — the word 'climate' refers to the prevailing levels of warmth, sunshine, rainfall and wind in a certain area over a period of time. These factors are monitored by scientists and the changes are recorded. Climate change can have an effect on the way we live and the plants that we can grow. Over the past twenty-five years, winter in the British Isles has become a little warmer (global warming).

Weather — the word 'weather' refers to the changes that occur in temperature, sunshine, wind and rainfall on a daily or monthly basis (as predicted by the weather forecast).

Plants will only grow within a certain temperature range. Some plants, such as grasses, can grow in a wide range of temperatures but many other plants need more specific conditions that are neither too hot nor too cold.

Protecting garden plants from bad weather

If you can shelter plants from wet, windy and cold weather, you will lengthen their growing season. Early and late salad crops, strawberries, cut flowers and tender bedding plants will benefit from shelter. A greenhouse can help to protect plants from spring and autumn frosts and provide an ideal environment to grow seeds and seedlings before planting them into the garden. On exposed sites a hedge or fence will help to protect plants from the wind. The use of movable trellising can also give valuable protection from the wind. Annual plants should be 'hardened-off' (put outside during the day time and brought in at night) until they are hardy and can be planted into open ground.

ACTIVITY SHEET 1 — RECORDING THE WEATHER

COLD	IDEAL	HOT
5°C (40°F)	10–25°C (50–75°F)	30°C (85°F)

Owl

Birds and wildlife

A well-established garden may provide a home for up to thirty different types of birds, six or more kinds of wild mammals and twelve different species of butterflies and moths.

Birds will feed on bugs and insects but they may also feed on fruit and vegetables, especially when they are ripe and ready to harvest. Garden birds provide interest and entertainment, colour, song and curiosity throughout the year. Some birds have adapted well to the habitat provided by buildings and plants in a town or country garden.

Goldfinch

Common visitors to our gardens include, among others:

Robin

Chaffinch

Swallow

Wren

Blackbird

House martin

Blue tit

Great tit

Sparrow

27

Occasionally you may see unfamiliar types of bird. It is a good idea to record the birds you see at different times of the year as this can act as a seasonal indicator, with certain birds arriving in the spring and leaving at the end of the summer, and others that only appear in winter.

Birds, hedgehogs, frogs and toads eat slugs, snails and insects, and in this way help to keep many garden pests under control.

Toad

Frog

Hedgehog

Creepy-crawlies

You will find many insects and other creepy-crawlies in the garden. Some walk, some crawl, some slide, some fly and some move very quickly. They are all fascinating little creatures to watch going about their daily business and it does help to know the 'goodies' from the 'baddies'. Perhaps it is wrong to group garden bugs as good or bad. They all have a purpose and it is only when certain insects start to eat flowers, fruit and vegetables that the gardener becomes aware and refers to them a 'pest' that must be controlled.

As a general rule of thumb, those that move quickly eat other insects. Those that move slowly eat plants and you need to keep an eye on them before they do a lot of damage. When the weather is warm and plants are lush and green, a quick leaf inspection will soon reveal any signs of infestation or nibbling. Generally the culprit will not be far away in the form of a slug, snail, caterpillar, aphid (greenfly and black fly) or insect larvae. An easily identified 'goody' is the ladybird, which devours damaging aphids, as does the ladybird's black larvae, identified by the orange spots on its body. The lacewing lays its eggs in caterpillars and the developing larvae eat their way out of the caterpillar's body — a rather gruesome but very effective method of control. Wasps may be considered a nuisance but they demolish vast quantities of greenfly. We like to encourage butterflies and moths into the garden because they look nice, but the yellow and green caterpillars of the cabbage white butterfly can soon consume a crop of cabbages. Another 'goody' is the fast moving centipede, but the slow moving black millipede (that when touched curls up like a spring) is a pest that eats plant roots, as does the woodlouse. Slugs and snails eat away at roots, stems and leaves.

Plants need protection from various pests that cause damage or disease and may destroy an entire crop. Nature ensures a fine balance between beneficial and harmful organisms, but occasionally conditions change, the balance is upset and a gardener has to resort to other methods (cultural and chemical) to control an infestation.

To maintain a balance and encourage birds and other small animals into the garden, care must be taken if using pesticides. The careless use of chemicals (e.g. slug pellets) may kill the pest but also harm birds and small animals.

Water skater

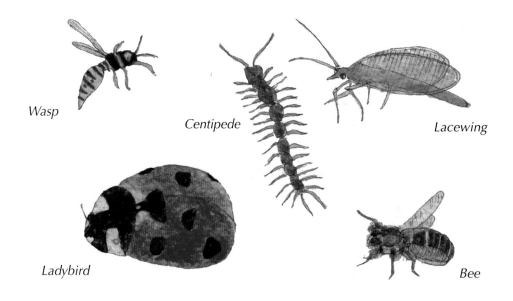

Wasp

Centipede

Lacewing

Ladybird

Bee

The best cultural method is to use a system of rotation whereby vegetable crops are grown on a different piece of the garden each year. This will prevent a build-up of any pest or disease. Plants and crops can also be covered with a fine fleece if necessary.

Caterpillars, slugs and snails will eat their way through an entire garden if they are not controlled.

ACTIVITY SHEET 2 — WILDLIFE IN YOUR GARDEN
ACTIVITY SHEET 6 — MAKING A BIRD TABLE
    AND FAT-BALL FOR FEEDING
ACTIVITY SHEET 7 — BUG SAFARI

Keeping a garden diary

Once you start gardening and growing plants you will notice that no two years are exactly the same. Nature can be so unpredictable. The changing seasons and the differences in the weekly weather pattern will affect plant growth, especially in northern areas. You can sometimes get a late, harmful frost when you thought that winter was over; or an unusually hot, dry summer with little rain; and sometimes the dry weather brings with it a plague of insects. There will be seasonal surprises that interrupt the normal pattern. Keep a note of these in your garden

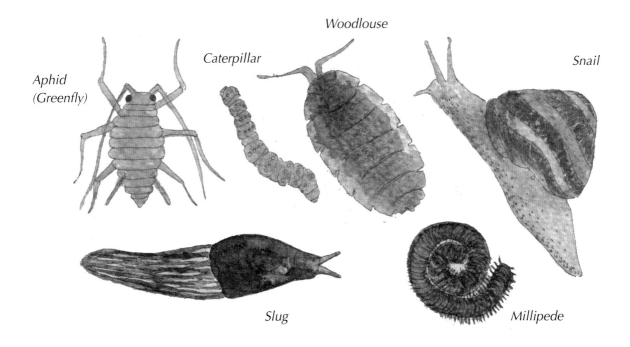

Aphid (Greenfly)   *Caterpillar*   *Woodlouse*   *Snail*   *Slug*   *Millipede*

diary so that you can plan and be ready should they occur again next year.

By recording the events that happen during the year, you will be more prepared for next year. For example, you will have a record of the date you planted seeds and when they germinated; when plants came into bud and flowered; what vegetable crops were planted where (crop rotation); whether there were any problems with pests and diseases and what methods you used for control; when migrant birds started to arrive in the spring ... and many other useful pieces of information that affected the garden and your gardening. Only record the things that interest you and always keep to a simple procedure. It is fascinating to look back at old diaries and compare one year with another.

ACTIVITY SHEET 3 — KEEPING A GARDEN DIARY

How Plants Grow

Poppies

The plant and how it functions

Each part of a plant has an important function.

Flowers

Flowers can look magnificent. Their job is to attract pollinating insects and produce seeds that ensure the survival of the plant. If you look closely at a flower it is easy to identify the parts. The flower is conveniently divided into male and female. The male anthers produce pollen (a powder-like substance), and the female stigma receives the pollen to fertilise the seeds, which are found in the ovary (seed pod). Have a look at a daffodil or lily flower and try to identify the male and female parts.

THE FLOWER

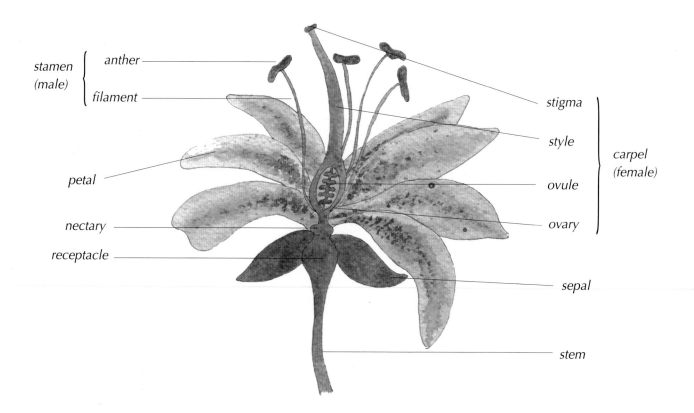

Leaves

Green leaves are important for photosynthesis, the process by which the plant manufactures simple sugars from water and carbon dioxide using the energy from sunlight; a plant can also make proteins for its natural growth.

Stem

The stem is for supporting the plant and keeping it upright. It also contains a system of microscopic tubes that allow water, nutrients and sugars to move around the plant. This process is known as transpiration (water movement) and translocation (movement of nutrients and sugars).

Hoverfly

Roots

Roots anchor a plant in the soil and absorb water and nutrients through their microscopic root hairs. A good root system is important for healthy growth. Damaged or poorly developed roots cannot absorb adequate water and nutrients for normal plant growth. The roots of a plant will rot and die in poorly drained, wet soil. Insect and fungal infestations can also destroy a plant's root system. The two main types of root system are the tap root (one solid, pointed root) and the fibrous root (a ball of hairy roots).

Seeds

A plant produces seeds that will germinate, grow and develop into another plant similar to itself. In the autumn many plants are getting ready for winter, some loose their leaves and 'go to sleep'; others will die and only their seeds remain to grow in the following year. This is the time to walk around the garden, park or countryside and look for seeds that can be collected, named and grown next year. The seeds that plants produce vary in size, shape, colour and quantity. Some are very small and look like dust, others are the size of sugar grains and dark in colour, some are quite big and easy to see. Gather seeds from flowers, shrubs and trees and try to grow them.

Photosynthesis

Plants require sunlight energy in order to build up sugars, starch and proteins from the simple inorganic minerals that they absorb through their roots. The process of photosynthesis requires the presences of chlorophyll (green pigment in plant leaves) and a supply of water and carbon dioxide before it can take place.

Plants that do not receive sufficient sunlight will not grow well and can turn pale green or yellow. This can be seen on any parts of a lawn that have been covered for a few days.

Plants do not grow well in areas shaded by hedges, trees or buildings. Not only do they get poor sunlight but the competition for water and nutrients will also affect them.

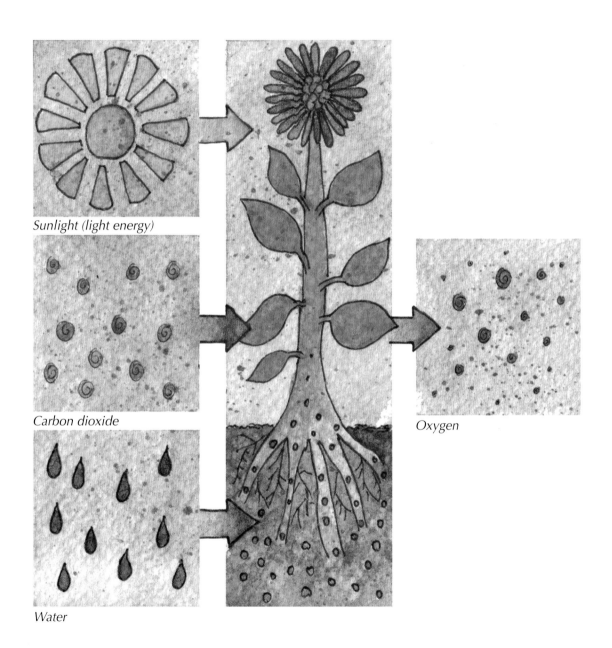

Sunlight (light energy)

Carbon dioxide

Water

Oxygen

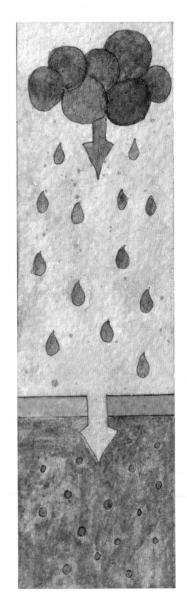
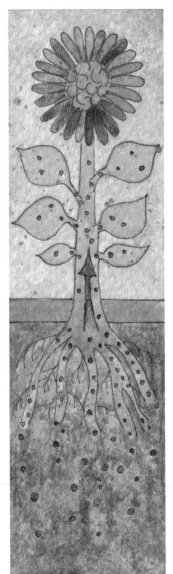
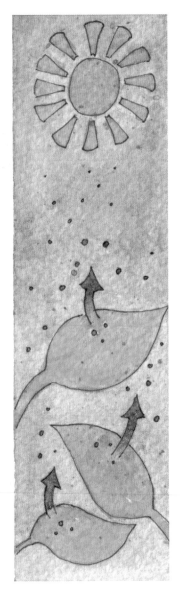

Transpiration

Water fills plant cells and gives the plant turgidity (shape and support), which helps to keep it standing upright. As water evaporates from the surface of the plant's leaves, more water is pulled through the plant. This process is known as transpiration. On a hot day plants will loose a lot of water by evaporation from their leaves. If the plant does not have enough water to replenish itself, it will wilt and become floppy.

Pot plants and plants in hanging baskets need careful watering and will quickly wilt if they are not watered regularly.

Translocation

Translocation is the movement of water and nutrients in one direction and the flow of sugars and proteins in the other.

Soil

All plants need soil to help them to grow. The soil provides an anchorage for plant roots and is where they obtain moisture and nutrients (food) to grow. Soil is a living substance. It contains many living things, from microscopic creatures that we cannot see and may not notice, to larger organisms like plants, insects and worms.

The type of soil depends on a number of factors that have accumulated over hundreds and thousands of years:

- the place where it is found (for example, on a mountain or in a valley)
- the original rocks from which it was formed
- the plants that have been growing in it
- the cultivations carried out by man over the centuries

Soil forms in layers. The main layers are the 'bedrock', from which all soils start; the 'sub-soil', smaller pieces of rock, stones and sand; and finally the 'top-soil'.

Top-soil is the living part of soil, which contains organic matter (humus), bacteria and fungi, as well as insects and earthworms.

Soil is a mixture of various materials:

1. Air and water — without air and water plants and soil organisms cannot live. Nutrients (plant food) dissolve in soil water, plants take up water by the process of transpiration (water movement in the plant).

2. Sand and grit ⎤ both formed from bed-
3. Stones and gravel ⎦ rock and sub-soil.

4. Humus and organic matter — the remains of living things that have gradually broken down in the soil.
5. Living organisms — insects, worms, plants fungus and bacteria etc.

Soil structure

This refers to how the particles of sand, clay and humus are held together, and it influences how much air, water and nutrients plants can access. Soil structure can be improved by adding organic matter (compost) to increase fertility, by ensuring good drainage and by digging over the soil in the autumn to allow the action of the weather (frost/rain) to break down the large clods of soil. Soil structure can be damaged by constantly walking over it, which causes compaction, particularly in wet weather.

Soil drainage

Plants will not grow well if the soil is too wet. Wet soils take longer to warm up in the spring and only certain plants will grow in boggy, damp soil. A wet area in the garden can be improved by increasing the drainage to let surplus water drain away. Plant roots need air to grow; where there is too much water in the soil, root development will be poor. Dig a ditch to carry water away from the area where plants are to be grown. A ditch dug across a lawn to one corner and then filled with sand can help garden drainage.

Soil pH

A soil may be acid or alkaline depending on how much lime (chalk) it contains. This can be measured and is known as the soil pH. The soil pH will determine what plants can be grown successfully in it. Rhododendrons and heathers grow well in acid soils, the type of soil found in moorland areas. For many vegetable crops this type of soil would be too acidic.

Soil pH can range from a low of pH 5.0 (acid) to a high of pH 8.0 (alkaline). The gardener aims to have a soil of pH 6.5 (slightly acid), which is ideal for most plants. You can check the pH of garden soil quite easily with a soil-testing kit (which you can buy at your local garden centre) or by noting what type of plants grow naturally in your garden and in the surrounding area.

Types of soil

CLAY SOIL

Clay soils are heavy, feel sticky and cold and can be moulded in the fingers. They are often very fertile but because they can be wet and cold, they take longer to warm up in the spring, so plants are slow to start their growth. A clay soil can be improved by good drainage and by adding sand and organic matter (compost and manure). Many plants don't like wet, cold, heavy soils but others, such as roses, can perform well in clay soils.

SANDY SOIL

Sandy soils are light, free draining and warm up quickly in the spring. They are easily worked but tend to dry out in the summer and have poor fertility, as minerals and nutrients are easily washed away (leached) in the free-draining conditions. Mediterranean plants grow well in light, sandy soils.

Peat
Peaty soils are often acidic, not very fertile, poorly drained and very dark brown in colour. Rhododendrons and heather's grow well in peaty soils.

Silt soil
Silt soils are moderately fertile. They can be moulded in the fingers, but they do not feel cold and sticky and they hold less water than clay. They can become easily compacted and can form a 'cap' or crust on the surface, which restricts plant growth. Hoeing will prevent this. Most plants will grow in silt soil.

The ideal soil is made-up of:
 22% water
 20% sand
 20% air
 15% silt
 10% clay
 8% unavailable water (trapped soil water is
   unavailable to plants)
 5% organic matter

Earthworms
There are many insects and organisms (small living things) that live in soil. They all have a purpose and there is a close balance between those that do good and those that are harmful.

Earthworms are entirely good (beneficial) animals, performing important functions in the soil. They increase its fertility and improve its structure

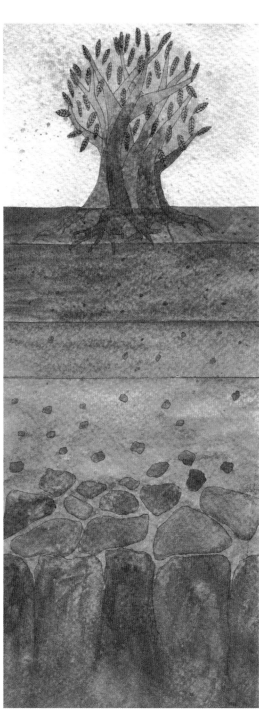

Top-soil

Sub-soil

Bedrock

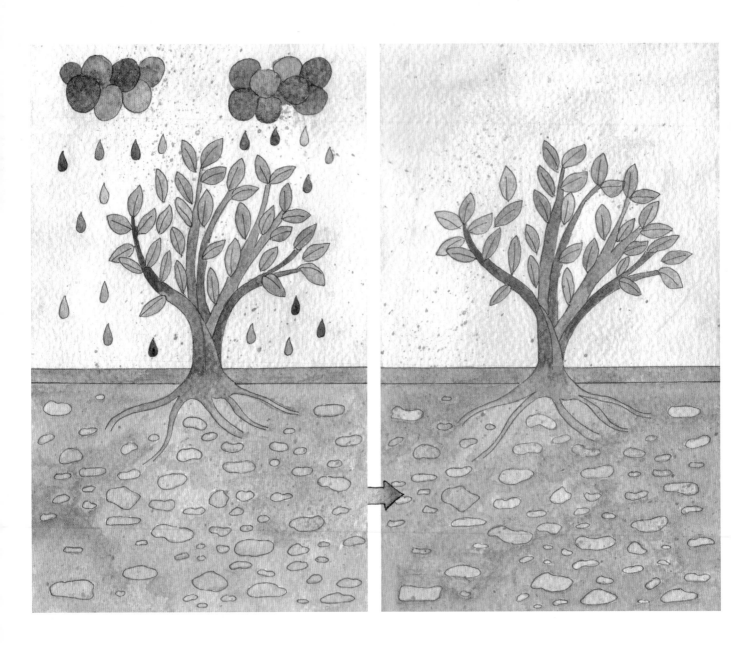

and aeration (air flow). They are valuable in treating waste, combating pollution and generally helping to rid the garden of leaves and other rotting vegetation. Worms take plant material and leaves down into the soil where it is eaten or rots and forms humus (which contains nutrients). The burrows formed by worms aerate and break up the soil, helping drainage and creating space for plants' roots to grow.

Charles Darwin, the nineteenth century scientist, studied earthworms and found that they are tremendous earthmovers. Over a period of thirty years he noticed that a path of stepping-stones that crossed his lawn had been completely covered by earth and disappeared from sight. This was due to the earthworms producing 'casts' (small piles of soil) all over the surface of the lawn and path area.

Earthworms belong to a group of invertebrate animals that have segmented bodies. There are twenty-eight species of earthworm in Britain and it is estimated that there are 7.5 million of them

Rhodedendron

per hectare. Garden compost contains small, red brandling worms, which are important as they break down raw plant material to make useful garden compost.

ACTIVITY SHEET 8 — EXPERIMENTING WITH SOIL

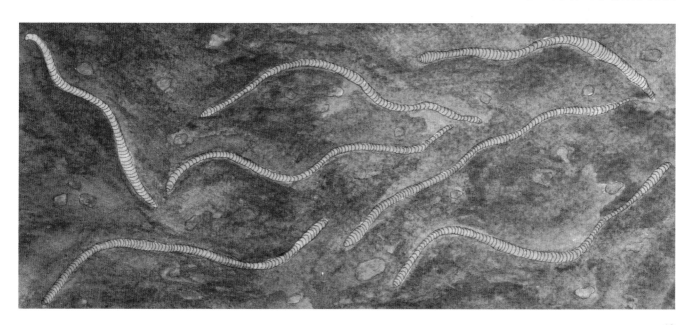

Plant food

All plants must have light, water, air, nutrients and warmth to grow. The best way to supply the food that plants need is to give them a good helping of garden compost or farm manure. This is sometimes called 'organic gardening'.

Garden compost — recycled garden rubbish

When plants die they decompose, which means they rot and disappear. Unwanted plant material can be collected and formed into a compost heap. The old plants and vegetation will rot and worms will start to turn it into compost, an organic, soil-like substance. Composting is a natural way of recycling unwanted plant and other organic material into plant food. Compost is a good soil improver and a good way of adding fertility to the garden. When compost is mixed with a heavy soil it makes it easier to work. Compost also aids moisture retention when added to sandy soils.

Minerals

Plants need minerals to grow. They are divided into two groups: major elements and trace elements.

MAJOR ELEMENTS

There are three elements that must be supplied for plants to grow well. In order of importance they are:

1. Nitrogen (N) — for general growth, proteins and chlorophyll.
2. Phosphorus (P) — for proteins, respiration, cell membranes and cell division. It is also important for plant root growth.
3. Potassium (K) — to balance water in cells and to give sweetness to fruit and help bud formation in fruit trees.

The three most important elements are N, P and K.

There are three other important minerals that plants need in small quantities:

4. Calcium (Ca) — for cell walls and membranes.
5. Magnesium (Mg) — for chlorophyll production.
6. Sulphur (S) — for protein formation.

TRACE ELEMENTS

The elements Boron (B), Copper (Cu), Manganese (Mn), Molybdenum (Mo), Iron (Fe), Iodine (I) and Selenium (Se) are also essential but are only required in very, very small amounts to keep plants in good health.

Mineral availability is dependent on the soil pH. If a soil is too acid or too alkaline then certain minerals and trace elements become 'locked-up' and will not be available to growing plants. Acid soils can be improved by adding lime (calcium) to change the soil pH and help make the minerals available for the plant roots to absorb.

Artificial (chemically made) fertilizer

Gardeners can buy balanced fertilizers to help plants grow and thrive. These can be granular or in liquid form. Growmore is a scientifically formulated granular fertilizer that contains the correct balance of N, P and K minerals for plant growth.

Remember, too much of one mineral can harm plants, for example, large quantities of nitrogen will give lush green growth but the plants will become weak and floppy and more susceptible to attack by pests and diseases. Also remember that

HOW TO MAKE GARDEN COMPOST

Just about anything that will rot down can make compost. Here are the ingredients for successful compost:

- Plant waste — green plants, roots, vegetable and soft fruit waste, garden rubbish
- Household waste — eggshells, tea bags, newspapers and organic things that will rot and decompose.
- Never compost — meat, fat, cooking oil, dairy products, bread, cakes and biscuits, synthetic fibres (nylon clothing), citrus fruit, wood or woody plants. Perennial weeds should only be composted if the heap can produce enough heat to kill them and you regularly turn the composting material.
- Warmth — cover the heap and keep it warm; use an old carpet.
- Air— turn the compost to let in air; this helps rubbish to decompose.
- Moisture — worms and living things need moisture (but not too wet).
- Soil organisms — add small amounts of garden soil to aid the composting process; the soil around waste plant roots will help.
- Time — turn the compost heap regularly and allow time for the organic materials to rot down. Compost is not smelly and will take a few months to form into a brown, crumbly substance that looks like soil and can be put back on to the garden.
- Two heaps — if you have the room, make two compost heaps/bins: one that has rotted down with compost ready for spreading on the garden and the other which can take new material to go through the composting process.

ACTIVITY SHEET 9 — MAKING A MINI COMPOST HEAP

if you add too much chemical fertilizer at one time you can kill plants.

Slow-acting fertilizers release nutrients over a period of six to twelve weeks. When mixed with compost, they are ideal for pot plants, containers and hanging baskets as they supply plant nutrients over more of the growing season.

Liquid fertilizers are suitable for house plants, grow-bags and all containers; always follow the instructions and don't give too much.

All About Plants!

Meconopsis

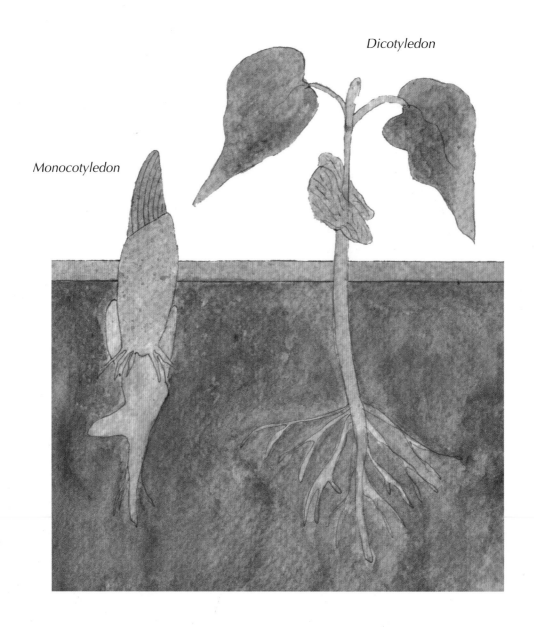

Dicotyledon

Monocotyledon

Plant names and families

Genus and species

The common name of a plant in one country may be quite different in another. This is confusing for botanists and gardeners so it is essential to have a universal system for classifying plants and living organisms. Carl Linnaeus, a Swedish naturalist (1707–1778), recognised the problem and methodically named and classified the whole living world in the Binomial System.

Linnaeus gave each living organism two names. The first (which may be likened to our surname) is the group or generic name, the 'genus'. The second name is the specific descriptive name, the 'species' that is given to each type of plant in the group (genus). This is like a Christian name in a family, but the same Christian name may appear in many other families (in other plant genus).

For example, there are three girls in the Smith family (the surname Smith is the genus or group name). They all have the same family surname but we identify the girls by their Christian names — Suzanne, Heather and Carol (species name). Within a plant genus we recognise individual plant types by their species name.

The plant kingdom is divided and subdivided according to the botanical characteristics of each plant. Two different species (Christian names) in the same genus (family surname) may be quite different from each other, as human siblings can be. One plant could be large and hardy whilst the other may be small and tender. This detailed information about plants allows the gardener to choose the right plant for the right place in the garden.

It is never easy to remember the proper (botanical) names of flowers, vegetables, shrubs or trees, but its common name may be easier to remember.

You may be attracted to a plant by its colour or shape, it may produce tasty fruit, it may be a plant that keeps appearing as a weed in the garden and is a nuisance. Some plants have a peculiar name and others a funny characteristic, which can help you to remember them. See if you can remember the common names of your favourite plants.

Varieties

A 'variety' is a naturally occurring and different form of a plant found in the wild. When plants adapt to a particular environment, a different variety can be produced.

Cultivars

These are plants that differ from the normal form of the species, but have been bred to do so by man.

Hybrids

Hybrid plants are produced by crossing two different parent plants. This is most common between two species of the same genus that are closely related. Good hybrids bring extra vigour and lustre to a plant; often hybrids will be bigger, brighter, sweeter and stronger than the normal plant.

When collecting seeds from a hybrid plant, remember that they will not breed true and the resulting plants can be very poor compared to their parent stock.

Dicotyledons and Monocotyledons

The plant kingdom is divided into two distinct groups — the Dicotyledons, which have two leaves at germination, and the Monocotyledons, which have one leaf at germination.

a. oak

b. sweet chestnut

c. silver birch

d. hawthorn

e. sycamore

f. large leaved lime

g. field maple

h. rowan

i. ash

j. wych elm

k. horse chestnut

l. beech

m. holly

n. alder

o. hazel

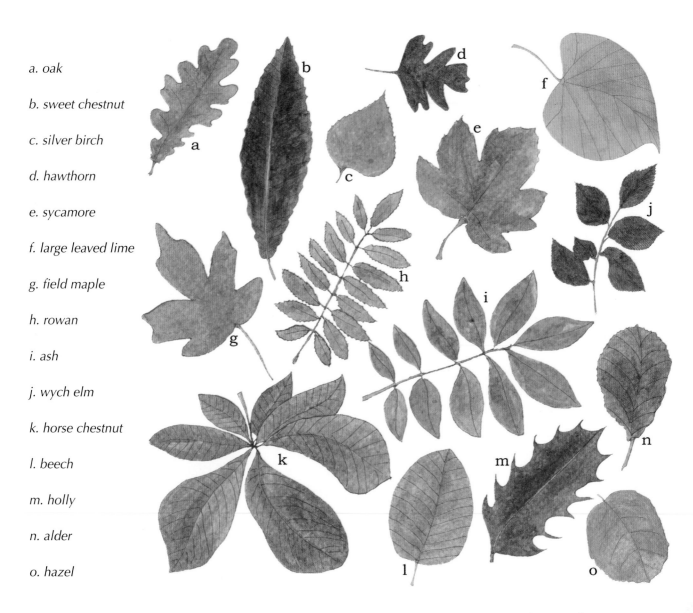

Leaves of common trees

Dicotyledons are the largest group of flowering plants. When a plant germinates (starts to grow) two thick leaves full of food feed the new growing plant until it is large enough to start producing its own food by the process of photosynthesis. The first leaves of a dicotyledonous plant are often broad and have a network of veins.

Monocotyledons have one seed leaf or cotyledon when they start to grow. The primary root soon dies and is replaced by a fibrous root system. Monocotyledonous plants are mainly herbaceous and have long, narrow leaves with parallel veins; grass is a monocotyledon.

ACTIVITY SHEET 10 — DRAWING AND NAMING PLANTS

Trees

Trees come in all shapes and sizes and generally need a lot of room to grow. A large tree may take forty to one hundred years to reach maturity and some can take even longer.

Trees are very beautiful and interesting. They support all sorts of wildlife, from animals and birds to insects, beetles, butterflies and bees. They also help to reduce our carbon footprint and clean up the atmosphere.

The leaf, bark and seeds (fruits) from each type of tree are different. Throughout the year leaves change colour from light green to dark green and finally to yellow, gold, brown and red, saving their best display until the autumn. Our parks and gardens would be poorer places without wonderful trees.

Trees and shrubs in the garden

Trees and shrubs enhance the garden and attract wildlife, but when planted in the wrong place, they can be a problem and take a lot of the garden's natural resources — light, water, nutrients and space.

To avoid any future problems when planting a garden tree or shrub, it is wise to know its mature size and select a suitable site. Don't plant shrubs

Sycamore leaves in autumn

Height in metres (feet)

60 (200)

50 (170)

40 (130)

30 (100)

20 (60)

10 (30)

Sweet Chestnut

Scots Pine

Beech

Douglas Fir   Oak   Rowan

53

or trees too close to buildings. Some trees remain small and will be no more trouble than a large shrub; this is the type of tree that is generally planted on a modern housing development.

Newly planted trees and shrubs need a lot of water to help them become established in the new site, so make sure that you prevent their roots and leaves from drying out.

Conifers (cone bearing trees) look good in a garden and some types can be used as hedging. They give year-round shape, colour and shelter.

ACTIVITY SHEET 11 — TREES

The garden lawn

Lawns can often have nearly as many weeds in them as grass. Count how many weeds are growing in half a square metre of a lawn; you will be surprised. Count how much bare ground there is between the grass plants and the weeds; generally there is quite a lot.

Most plants found in a lawn are green, and in the spring when everything is growing well in the moist, warm conditions they all look fine, but by mid summer it may be a different sight. When the weather is sunny and dry, well-rooted lawn grass will continue to grow, but shallow-rooted weeds, including some weed grasses and moss, cannot reach down into the soil for moisture and they will stop growing and may die. Many weeds will be past their main growing period by mid summer and may be naturally dying-off. This is when the lawn looks a brownish, yellow-green colour. The darker green patches are the areas where the true, well-established lawn grass is still growing.

A good raking in the autumn and early spring will remove moss, debris and some shallow-rooted weeds. Raking the lawn will also help to aerate the ground and stimulate grass growth. Perennial weeds in the lawn are a more difficult problem. They have to be either dug out individually or treated with a selective herbicide. Lawns need a dressing of a balanced fertilizer in the spring and summer. Spring is a good time to reseed any bare patches in the lawn.

Powered grass-cutting machinery and sharp, cutting implements are dangerous and children should not use them. Any person using a new piece of equipment for the first time should be closely supervised. Always trim the edges of a lawn to make it look neat and tidy. It also removes places where slugs, snails and other harmful insects can hide.

What is a weed?

A weed is a plant growing in the wrong place. For example, a nice-looking flower growing in the middle of some vegetables is called a weed because the gardener doesn't want it to be there and it can become a nuisance. When you walk around the garden, particularly in the late spring and early summer, you will notice that any bare ground soon becomes covered with weeds. Weeds can grow very rapidly and start to compete with other plants. Weeds can be removed quite easily with a hoe or by loosening the soil with a hand fork and pulling them out. Put annual weeds on the compost heap.

ACTIVITY SHEET 12 — IDENTIFYING COMMON WEEDS

How long do plants live?

As well as being classified according to their general make-up, plants are grouped according to the length of time they continue growing — in other words, how long they live.

Annuals

Annuals, often referred to as 'bedding plants', complete their life cycle from germination to seed production and then die in one year. They are divided into two types:

- Hardy annuals — these plants can survive periods of cold weather when grown outside.
- Half-hardy annuals — these plants grow outside but may die in cold weather.

Biennials

Biennial plants need two years to complete their life cycle. The seed germinates in the first year and then grows. It lives over winter and the following year produces flowers and seeds before dying.

Primula

Several species of Primula

Right: Perennial plants

Foxglove, turnip, swede and carrot are examples of biennial plants. Crops of turnip, swede, carrot and beetroot are harvested as a vegetable at the end of the first year of growth, when they have stored food in their root (the part that we eat) before a flower is produced.

Perennials

Perennials are hardy plants that continue to grow year after year. Trees and shrubs are perennials. They have permanent woody stems (trunks) above ground and start new growth each year from over-wintering buds. Their durability enables them to grow to a great size.

HERBACEOUS PLANTS

Gardeners refer to some perennial plants as 'herbaceous'. These plants die back to soil level every winter but re-grow the following spring, often larger and better than before. When such plants have grown too big for their original place in the garden, the clump can be lifted (dug up) and divided into two or more pieces and transplanted. This can be carried out every three or four years either in the late autumn or early spring when the plant is dormant (not actively growing). It can take a couple of years for perennial plants that have been grown from seed to mature and flower. Some herbaceous perennials cannot stand low winter temperatures and need to be protected from frost; cover the ground with straw or mulch (compost or wood chips).

ROCK GARDEN PLANTS

Most rock plants are perennials. They are often small and demand good drainage and sunshine.

Many 'Alpine' plants are from mountainous areas and are very delicate and pretty when they flower. Rock plants can stand the cold but many do not like to be wet in the winter and need to be protected from rain in the colder months or they will rot and die. Rock garden plants make wonderful miniature gardens that can be grown in stone, wood and plastic containers. Small rock gardens look attractive in a sunny corner where the enthusiast can keep a tremendous number of these delicate little Alpine plants in a small area.

Evergreen and deciduous plants

Some trees and shrubs retain their leaves throughout the year: these are known as 'evergreens'. Holly, ivy, yew and pine trees are examples of evergreens. Trees and shrubs that lose their leaves each autumn are known as 'deciduous'. Forsythia, rose and hydrangea are examples of deciduous plants.

The evergreen trees in the foreground contrast with deciduous trees in the background

Growing Plants

Sow your seeds at regular intervals and label them

Growing your own plants can bring a lot of pleasure, especially when flowers bloom and vegetables are harvested for a meal. The methods a gardener can use to grow (propagate) plants includes sowing seeds, taking cuttings and planting bulbs.

Growing plants from seed

You will find that garden seeds, for both flowers and vegetables, are quite cheap to buy, generally under £2.00 per packet from a garden centre, nursery or hardware shop. You will be surprised how many plants you can get from one packet of seeds. Some seeds are very small; be careful when you are sowing as they can easily spill and be wasted.

It is quite easy to grow plants from seed providing you follow a few basic rules. There will be some information on the back of the seed packet to help you get the best results. Read these instructions before you start; you will find them helpful.

To germinate seeds (get them growing) five things are needed:
1. A rest (dormancy) period — if you buy a packet of seeds this will have been done by the seed collector before the treated, dried seed is put in the packet.
2. Moisture
3. Warmth
4. Light
5. Air (oxygen)

Warmth and moisture are the two most important factors needed for germination after seeds have had a dormant (rest) period. If conditions are too cold and wet, seeds will rot and die. This is particularly common with sweetcorn, beans and courgette seeds when they are sown in unfavourable conditions.

One way to remember what seeds need is WIGWAM:

W — what
I — induces
G — germination?
W — warmth
A — air
M — moisture

Frost and cold weather will also kill seedlings, so it is important to protect them at certain times of the year. When the weather is cold, cover tender plants or take them into the house or greenhouse where they will be warm and can continue growing until the weather improves.

Be a wise gardener and don't sow vegetable seeds all at once; save some in the packet for a few weeks later when you can sow a second crop. This works well with carrots, radishes and lettuces. By sowing at regular intervals the plants won't all mature at the same time and a succession of crops can be harvested over a longer period.

Remember to always label the seed you have sown, whether directly into the ground or into seed trays or pots. The label will remind you what has been planted.

ACTIVITY SHEET 13 — SOWING SEEDS

Pricking-out and planting-out

When any seeds that were sown into pots or trays have germinated, and before the seedlings have grown too big, they should be transplanted into bigger pots and trays that will allow them to continue to grow naturally without too much competition. If you intend to plant new seedlings directly into open ground, they need to be put outside for a few days to 'harden-off' and should only be planted outside if conditions are favourable — not wet or frosty. If seedlings are left too long in their original seed pot/tray they will become weak and floppy and can die from fungal diseases.

Hardening-off

It is unwise to take plants directly from a protected, warm environment and put them straight into the garden. Give them time to acclimatise or 'harden-off' by putting the trays outside during the day and either bringing them inside or covering them with horticultural fleece at night.

ACTIVITY SHEET 14 — PRICKING-OUT AND
PLANTING-ON
ACTIVITY SHEET 15 — GROWING SUNFLOWERS

Collecting seeds

The seeds produced from garden plants come in all shapes and sizes. Many flower and weed seeds are so small, they are almost like dust and you barely notice them. Other seeds are large and easy to see: horse chestnut trees produce conkers and oak trees produce acorns. Some seeds are hidden inside fruit, like the pips in apples and raspberries or the stones in cherries and plums.

When plants mature they often produce seeds that will germinate and grow in the following year if conditions are favourable. Of course some seeds, such as nuts and cereal grains, never get the opportunity to grow as they are stored and eaten by animals and humans as food.

Autumn is the best time to collect seeds from the garden and you will be surprised and fascinated by the number and variety of seeds to be collected from small plants and trees. Remember that some plants may not breed true to type as the parent plant may have been a hybrid.

ACTIVITY SHEET 16 — SEED COLLECTING

Hardy annual seeds

These can be sown directly into the open soil when weather conditions are warm enough in April and May. There are some rules to remember to ensure that you will be successful:

- Never sow into wet, cold, muddy soil as many seeds will rot.
- Don't sow too deeply as the green shoots will struggle to push through the soil.

- When sowing into open ground, carefully sprinkle the seed on to the prepared soil surface and lightly rake it over; don't sow too densely and don't use the entire packet in case you have a failure and have to sow again.
- Once the seeds have germinated and are growing well, they can be 'thinned-out' to give those that you leave more room to grow into strong, healthy plants.
- Hardy annual seeds can also be sown into pots and then 'pricked-out' when the seedlings are growing. This means transplanting the seedlings into a larger pot, tray or into the garden, so that they can carry on growing without competition from other plants. The process of pricking-out may be carried out several times before an individual plant reaches its final growing place.

Half-hardy annual seeds

These are best sown into seed trays or pots and kept in a heated greenhouse or on a bright windowsill in the house. Once they start to grow the seedlings can be 'pricked-out' into growing trays or pots where they will continue to grow and get stronger. Plants should not be transferred to the garden until all possibility of frost has past and they are strong and growing well.

Perennial seeds

Perennial border plants can also be cheaply grown from seed, but you will have to wait a year or so for them to mature and become strong, colourful plants. Established perennial herbaceous plants can be dug up and split every three or four years. Each of these pieces can be planted in a new position and will grow into a new plant.

Transfer young plants to the garden when they are strong enough

Growing trees and shrubs from seed

Sowing time for tree and shrub seeds will vary. Some seeds need to be sown in the autumn and 'frozen' during the winter months to shock them into growth next spring. Other seeds will grow naturally after a period of dormancy.

Collect some large seeds from an oak or horse chestnut tree and plant them in some reasonably sized pots outside. Next year, when they have germinated, they can be replanted in a more suitable spot.

Taking cuttings

When conditions are right, many plants are able to grow from either a piece of stem, leaf or root and produce a new plant; this is known as 'vegetative reproduction' or 'taking cuttings'. Taking cuttings is a good and cheap way of producing new plants that will be identical to the parent stock. To achieve success take cuttings from new, soft stems of healthy plants that are growing vigorously between May and July. These 'softwood' cuttings can be taken from fuchsias, geraniums and hydrangea and rarely disappoint. Any healthy new shoots can be cut from just under a leaf joint (node), potted into moist, light compost and left in a warm position to grow. When cuttings have rooted and are growing well, they can be pricked-out into larger pots and treated like any tender young plant.

Cuttings taken from 'semi-ripe' or 'mature' woody plants, such as viburnum and escallonia, should be taken in the autumn and dug into well-drained open soil. Not all the cuttings will survive but some will over-winter before they root next spring. These 'hardwood' cuttings can be more difficult to propagate. Root and leaf cuttings are also difficult and require experience and some skill to master.

ACTIVITY SHEET 17 — TAKING CUTTINGS

Taking a cutting

Growing spring bulbs

Spring bulbs are easy to grow and, providing a few simple rules are followed, hardly anything can go wrong. When choosing daffodil bulbs for potting, go for a variety with short, strong stems that will support the flower heads and not become floppy. Hyacinth bulbs do not vary greatly in size and the large flowers generally need support; smaller bulbs tend to support themselves better. Bulbs like damp, free-draining soil. They are planted in the autumn and stored over winter ready to flower in spring.

Pot-planted bulbs can be a disappointment when they are not stored correctly. A warm, dark cupboard is not a good place for bulb storage as they will dry out, with the leaves and stems becoming long, yellow and floppy. For the best results, place the pots in a cool, well-ventilated, dark area or make a 'plunge-bed' outside. A plunge-bed allows bulbs to grow naturally and their flowering can be controlled. A strong cardboard box stored in a dry cold garage or shed will also do, but keep your eye on the plants to ensure that they don't grow weak and floppy.

Bulbs grow slowly during the winter months, and in February, when green shoots are showing, they should be removed from the plunge-bed/store and given plenty of light. A combination of temperature and light will determine when the bulbs flower. High temperatures and low light levels will produce poor, floppy plants. The best results are achieved from natural growth in a cool, well-lit area. A steady increase in temperature and good light will advance the flowering date and produce strong plants.

ACTIVITY SHEET 18 — GROWING SPRING BULBS IN POTS

Spring bulbs

Garden Groceries

Sow seeds into shallow drills

The vegetable garden

Fresh vegetables are nutritious and easy to grow. They are tasty and contain vitamins and minerals for a healthy, balanced diet. A variety of vegetables can be grown from seed and include peas, beans, leeks, onions, cabbages, celery, carrots, marrow/courgettes and salad crops such as radishes, lettuces and tomatoes.

A vegetable garden needs deep, fertile, well-drained soil with plenty of light in a sunny position. Most vegetable crops are grown in long rows. Straight lines of plants look neat and tidy and are easy to weed.

Bed system and crop rotation

You can sow or transplant your vegetables into a small plot or 'bed' (1.5–2 m / 5–6 $^{1}/_{2}$ ft in size). A bed is simple to cultivate and means the gardener can avoid walking on the prepared ground. Growing vegetables in this way has several advantages for smaller gardens. The crops that you plant can be easily moved to a different position every year (crop rotation) within the plot or bed system, which helps to prevent a build-up of pests and diseases.

Once the plants have been harvested, compost or manure can be worked into the bed in preparation for the next crop. This practice will lead to good soil fertility and increasing yields.

A series of 'veggie-beds' gives a delightful patchwork effect to the garden, which is both attractive and practical.

Sowing vegetable seeds

Most seeds can be sown directly into a well-prepared seedbed in April or early May, depending on the weather conditions. Sow seeds into shallow drills (a straight row approximately 2 cm / 1 in deep) and lightly rake the soil to cover them. For the best results allow plenty of space between plants when thinning-out or transplanting seedlings:

- Cabbage 30–40 cm (12–16 in) apart

- Lettuce 20 cm (8 in) apart

• Leeks 20 cm (8 in) apart

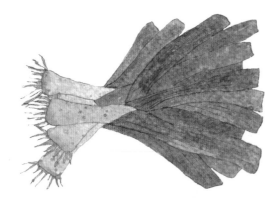

• Carrots and radishes 5–10 cm (2–4 in) apart

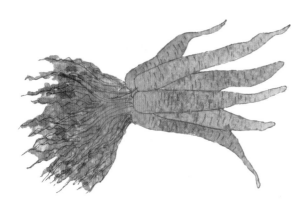

Also allow approximately 30 cm (12 in) between the rows. This will help when you hoe to control weeds.

Tomato plants can be planted outside but not until June when all possibility of frost has passed. They will need a warm, sunny site with plenty of liquid feeding for a good crop. Most varieties need to be tied back and supported with canes. Don't over water or let tomato plants dry out.

Courgette and marrow seeds must have warm conditions to germinate. They need plenty of space to grow, at least a square metre (3 ft) per plant. Sow individual seeds into pots and keep them in a glass/green house. Only transplant strong plants to the garden after they have been hardened-off and all chance of frost has past. Courgettes like fertile soil.

Growing potatoes

There are many varieties of potato, but they are classified into three distinct groups according to the time of harvesting:

- First early potatoes — these are harvested in early summer and known as new potatoes.
- Second early potatoes — these are harvested in mid to late summer.
- Main crop potatoes — these are harvested in the autumn and generally produce the biggest yield.

Dig plenty of compost into the garden before planting potatoes as they require well-drained, rich, deep soil and moisture to grow well. Some varieties are susceptible to blight (an airborne fungal disease) but if the crop is harvested when the leaves (haulm) start to shrivel and change colour, a reasonable yield can be expected.

PLANTING 'SEED' POTATOES (POTATO TUBER)

A 'tuber' is a swollen underground root or stem used for the storage of food (carbohydrate), and it produces shoots for a new plant. The tuber is the part of the potato we eat and it can also be used as a 'seed' for growing new potato plants. Seed potatoes should be 'chitted' (have short green shoots) before they are planted in mid to late April when the garden soil is warm. To chit seed potatoes, place them in a shallow tray in a cool, light area and protect them from frost. Soon the potato will produce strong, green, healthy shoots that are ready for planting.

Make a shallow trench about 10–12 cm (4–5 in) deep with a garden rake, or draw a hoe in a straight line across the plot, and place a seed potato every 20–30 cm (8–12 in). Mark the rows and cover the seed potatoes with soil. Allow half a metre (1 1/2 ft) between each row.

As the green shoots emerge, 'earth-up' the soil around each plant (using a draw hoe) to form a ridge of earth that covers the new, small shoots of the growing potatoes. This should be done two or three times and about fifteen to twenty-five days apart, depending on growth, with the soil ridge reaching 25 to 30 cm (10–12 in) in height. This procedure helps to protect the growing plants from frost and will keep weeds down.

HARVESTING POTATOES

This will depend on the variety that was planted, the season's growing conditions and the size of the potatoes (tubers) after they have been growing for ten to twelve weeks. Early potatoes can be lifted (dug up) from mid to late June when the leaves may still be green. The main harvest for potatoes is generally in the autumn, in September and October before the ground gets too wet.

Store potatoes in a cool, dark, dry place in a sack or large, strong paper bag; never store potatoes that are wet or diseased and don't use plastic bags, as the tubers will sweat, rot and go green.

Planting vegetables in a flower garden

If you only have a small garden don't give up on growing vegetables as they can be planted in a mixed border with flowering bedding plants. Parsley, lettuce, leeks and beetroot can look very attractive mixed with flowers.

Growing vegetables in plastic bags and containers

An alternative for those who don't have a vegetable garden, but would like to grow some fresh vegetables or salad crops, is to grow them in a bag or large container. A grow-bag can be purchased quite cheaply or you can make your own veggie-bags from plastic shopping bags and compost with some added fertilizer (as described in activity sheet 20).

Try to grow plants from seed (as explained in activity sheet 13), but you can also buy good quality plants from a garden centre or nursery quite cheaply.

The best results are obtained from bags and containers placed in a sheltered, sunny position with plenty of light. Once planted, the grow-bag should not be moved. Ensure that the bag or container has adequate drainage holes and water the plants regularly. Check for pest damage, especially slugs and snails.

Tomatoes, lettuce, herbs, courgettes and leeks give an excellent return for your efforts and are well worth a try. Potatoes should not be grown in bags as the tubers do not get sufficient compost/soil cover and they will turn green. Potatoes grown in a bucket or barrel can produce an excellent crop in or out of season.

ACTIVITY SHEET 20 — GROWING PLANTS IN
     SHOPPING BAGS
ACTIVITY SHEET 19 — GROWING POTATOES IN A BUCKET

Controlling vegetable pests

Insects and caterpillars love eating tasty vegetable and salad crops. One easy way to protect tender young plants is to place a plastic juice bottle, with the top and bottom cut off, over each plant. When the plants have grown beyond the height of the plastic bottles, remove the bottles and cover the crop with fine garden fleece. If you use this method to protect lettuce plants, the plastic bottles need to be shorter.

There are a number of insect pests that tuck into carrots and plants of the cabbage family. Once their eggs hatch, the grubs can destroy a crop without you knowing it. Using a crop rotation system can help to prevent a crop failure. Pests such as the carrot root fly can only fly at a certain height, and if their flight path is blocked they will have difficulty reaching the carrot crop to lay their eggs. The carrot fly also has a strong sense of smell, so try planting onions or some herbs either side of a row or bed of carrots.

Alternatively you can secure fleece over an area where seeds have been sown. Remember that germinating weed seeds will also grow well under a fleece so you will have to weed every now and again.

ACTIVITY SHEET 21 — WHAT ARE MY
     VEGETABLES WORTH?
ACTIVITY SHEET 22 — GARDEN VEGETABLE SOUP

Growing herbs

Garden herbs are used to add flavour to cooking, to make refreshing herbal drinks and for medici-

nal purposes. Herbs are quite easy to grow. A small herbal garden constructed with pots and containers of various sizes on a patio or back yard can look good and be fun to care for.

To grow herbs needs no special skill; a fertile, free-draining soil or compost will give good results. When growing herbs in containers you need to ensure that they drain well, are watered regularly and are given fertilizer or liquid feed during the growing months, and they will do well. Don't over water the plants; only water when the soil or compost feels dry.

Herbs can be grown from seed or purchased from a garden centre in small pots and transplanted later. Some herbs such as parsley, basil, coriander and dill are annuals that need to be sown or purchased every year; rosemary, thyme and sage are perennial plants and will produce usable leaves for several years if they are well looked after. Mint and lemon balm will grow rapidly and can take over the herb garden (invasive plants) once they have become established and their growth is not contained. Chives are a good flavoursome substitute for onion; when grown in a pot on a windowsill their grass-like leaves can be produced throughout the year.

Herbs grow rapidly and their leaves should be trimmed regularly to produce a compact, bushy plant. Sage, rosemary and thyme plants should be trimmed near the end of the growing season with scissors or garden shears; this will help to prevent the plant from becoming too large and woody.

Pests and diseases are not usually a problem when growing herbs and if planted near certain vegetables, the smell of the herb will deter a pest from attacking the crop. Generally herbs will only suffer from pests and diseases if the growing conditions are poor; aphids and red spider mite can cause problems in some seasons.

Plan to have your herb garden or potted herbs near to the house so you can quickly pop outside and gather fresh herbs when you are cooking.

Growing fruit

Britain, particularly Scotland, is noted for the 'soft fruit' it produces: raspberries, strawberries, loganberries, blackberries (brambles) and blackcurrants can all be successfully grown in the garden and will provide delicious fruit from June to October. Apples, pears, peaches, apricots, plums, cherries, damsons and grapes are also commonly grown by gardeners, but some fruit needs special attention and protection from difficult weather conditions and marauding insects in order to produce a good crop.

Strawberries, raspberries and most of the soft fruits will produce a crop within a year of planting. Fruit grown on bushes, like the blackcurrant, will take a little longer to establish and fruit trees, such as apple trees, may take a few years to produce fruit, but it will be worth waiting for. Many modern varieties will not take up much space and they can be grown in a confined area. If space is a problem in your garden, fruit trees can be trained to grow against a wall or fence.

Fresh fruit from the garden is tasty and good for you. Try growing some strawberry plants in a pot, barrel, grow-bag or a two-litre plastic milk container with the bottom cut off and drainage holes at the other end. They will need to be watered regularly in early summer when the fruit is developing, but after the fruit has been picked, the plants can be left in the container and only checked over a couple of times during the rest of the year; don't let the plants dry out!

ACTIVITY SHEET 23 — FRESH FRUIT TASTING

Plants in Pots

House plants

Pot plants brighten up the home and last for a reasonable length of time if they are cared for properly. Unfortunately many pot plants are killed by kindness through over watering, which drowns the plant, or by keeping them too warm — a cool room is fine for most plants.

All plants need light but many are not happy in direct sunlight as it can scorch their leaves. If you cannot read a book in a room then there is a strong possibility that the light level is insufficient for the plant and it will soon suffer.

Pot plants will dry out if placed too close to a heater or radiator. Water plants regularly but only when the potting compost feels dry or when the leaves begin to wilt, once every ten days is generally adequate but this will depend on the temperature and whether the plant is growing or in a resting phase. During the winter watering once every two or three weeks is generally sufficient.

Most pot plants grow between April and September and will require some nutrients during this period. Liquid feeding with a tomato-type fertiliser should be OK, but for certain plants, especially the unusual and exotic types, specially formulated plant feeds are available. Winter flowering plants may need feeding between October and March. Plants purchased from a nursery or garden centre may not need additional fertiliser as sufficient nutrient is contained in the potting compost.

Re-pot house plants every two years, earlier if the plant has outgrown its pot. Re-potting is best done in the spring using John Innes No. 2 potting compost. Some pot plants are perennial and hardy and can be planted in the garden when they have finished flowering (spring bulbs).

Pot plants like to be outside during the warm summer months — it's like a summer holiday for them. A good wash of soft summer rain will clean their leaves and refresh the whole plant and they will look a lot better for it. Remember to water them and spray the leaves in the evening when the weather is hot and dry. Make sure that you don't forget them and make a note in your diary to bring them inside again before the first frost. It is good practice to re-pot plants before bringing them inside for the winter.

Pot-plant pests

Greenfly, whitefly and mealy bug produce a sticky residue that covers plant leaves. This sticky honey-dew attracts a sooty mould and soon plant leaves look dull and dirty. Act quickly as soon as you spot any greenfly or other pest problem. Spray the plant with soapy water or a systemic insecticide at the first sign of trouble. Put the soapy water into a hand sprayer and spray the plant all over, holding the container approximately 30 cm (1 ft) from the plant. Take the plant outside to spray it and bring it back inside once the foliage is dry. It may be necessary to repeat the spray treatment every ten days to ensure all emerging bugs are

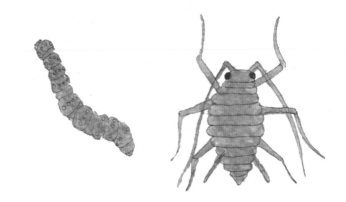

killed. If you are using a pesticide, remember to read the instructions on the spray container and wash your hands carefully after using it. Children should not use any pesticides.

Some insects, such as vine weevil and chafer grubs, will attack the roots of a pot plant, causing it to wilt and look as if it requires water. A gentle pull on the main stem of the plant will generally indicate the presence of any root problems. If the roots have been eaten away the plant will become unstable and unable to support itself. When the potting compost is examined, small creamy-white grubs with small brown heads may be found. If this is the case it is generally too late for any curative treatment. Destroy all the grubs you find and put the old compost on to open ground in the garden, where birds can eat any remaining grubs. Wash the remaining roots of the plant to ensure all grubs are removed and re-pot the plant into new, clean compost. With care the plant may survive.

PCT is a good way to remember how to care for your pot plants:
   P — position
   C — care
   T — tips

- Position: Place your pot plant in a well-lit place away from direct sunlight, draughts and heaters. Ideal temperature 10–15 °C (50–60 °F). Stand pots outside during warm summer weather and occasionally spray them with water.
- Care: Keep your pot plant moist and avoid over watering at all times. In winter do not allow the pot to dry out and only water occasionally. Feed pot plants regularly during the summer and spring when they are growing. Treat or discard any diseased plants.
- Tips: Remove any faded flowers to encourage new ones. Gently wipe dust from shiny leaves.

Outdoor containers

Even if you don't have a garden there is always a place where a pot or some sort of container, such as a window box, trough or tub can be filled with plants to add colour to an otherwise dull area in a back yard or patio. Containers dry out quicker than open ground and need regular watering, especially during hot, dry periods.

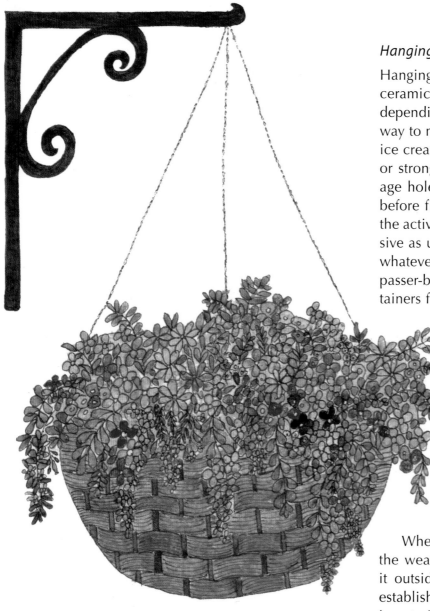

Hanging baskets

Hanging baskets can be made of wire, cane, ceramics or plastic. They can vary in price depending on size and style. A cheap and easy way to make a hanging 'basket' is to use a plastic ice cream or milk container suspended with wire or strong cord. Make sure there are some drainage holes in the bottom of the plastic container before filling it in the same way as described on the activity sheet. The result can be just as impressive as using a purpose-made basket. Ensure that whatever you use is safe and will not fall on a passer-by. Hanging baskets and suspended containers full of plants can be heavy and will cause damage if not secure.

The plants used for a hanging basket need not be expensive and you can grow them yourself. The best effect is obtained from trailing plants that can be planted around the top and through the side of the basket. Trailing petunias, surfinias, geraniums, lobelia and nasturtiums will look delightful. Other colourful plants like fuchsia will add height and colour to the decoration.

When the basket is planted-up, protect it from the weather for a week or two before you hang it outside for the summer. Once the plants are established and have hardened-off, the main task is watering — twice a day during hot, dry periods. Never let hanging baskets dry out as the plants will suffer and look scruffy.

ACTIVITY SHEET 24 — HANGING BASKETS

Window boxes and containers

TYPE AND SIZE OF CONTAINER

Plant containers come in many sizes, shapes and colours and can be made from a variety of materials: clay, stone, wood, metal and plastic. They need not be expensive and you can make your own 'planters' from a 2 litre (2 quart) plastic milk container, a large biscuit tin, a wooden box or any other water-resistant container that can hold a depth of at least 15 cm (6 in) of soil. The bottom of the container must have drainage holes to prevent waterlogging and sufficient compost/soil to support the growing plants; some small stones in the bottom will assist drainage. Mix a small amount of long-acting fertilizer (follow makers recommendations) with soil/compost. This will supply plant food throughout the growing season.

The container will require regular attention; watering, dead-heading and removing dead and diseased plants will help to keep the display fresh. During the season occasionally weed and loosen the soil around growing plants. It is important to treat any pests as soon as they appear.

WHAT PLANTS TO USE

When choosing plants for your container, careful consideration is needed. Will the plants grow well together? Do they prefer sun or shade? How much room do they need and when will they flower? Thinking carefully about all this information will help to make a better display. Generally a selection of bedding plants from the garden centre will provide a lasting bright display.

PALLET GARDENS

Groups of pots and other containers of different shapes and sizes can be arranged on a wooden pallet (approx. 1 m / 3 ft square) for a wonderful show of colour. The procedure is similar to flower arranging as you can move the pots and containers around to get the best effect. A pallet display is a simple and easy way of producing your own small colourful garden. It can also be used to produce herbs, salad crops and soft fruit such as strawberries.

ACTIVITY SHEET 25 — MAKING A PALLET GARDEN

Pelegonium

A Seasonal Guide to Gardening

Gardening activities

In this chapter you will find an introduction to each month in the gardening year, along with suggestions of appropriate tasks to undertake. Some of the activities on the accompanying CD are continuous and should be carried on through each month of the year. These are:

1. Recording the weather
2. Wildlife in your garden
3. Keeping a garden diary

Some are seasonal activities that should be carried out around the time indicated. The monthly suggestions are flexible, but you should aim to undertake certain activities during the appropriate season, e.g. you could do a January activity in February or December instead:

- Winter — December, January, February
- Spring — March, April, May
- Summer — June, July, August
- Autumn — September, October, November

Although they are allocated to a particular month in the following seasonal programme, some of the activities can be carried out whenever you have a spare moment and want to have fun. These activities are marked with *. The most important thing is to enjoy your gardening year.

January

January

January is generally a quiet month in the garden and apart from the odd bit of tidying-up that gardeners always find to do, such as looking for fences and trellis that need repairing and any potential hazards, it appears that not much is happening. But nature is always working. The weather can be grey, wet and cold with some frost and snow for good measure.

Most plants are in their mid-winter slumber but you will find some signs of life in the garden; it may be a winter flowering shrub (viburnum) or small, bright crocus flowers, snowdrops and early daffodils that start to poke their green shoots through the soil. And this is the time of year to observe the wildlife, birds and animals that visit a garden.

Plants need moisture, warmth and light to grow. To prove that seeds can grow in the winter, place one or two bean or pea seeds in a jar along with some damp cloth or kitchen roll and put the jar on the windowsill; keep the contents moist and see what happens.

ACTIVITY SHEETS
*4. GARDEN TOOLS
*5. HAZARDS IN THE GARDEN
*6. MAKING A BIRD TABLE AND FAT-BALL FOR FEEDING

Siskin

Dunnock

Greenfinch

ebruary

February

'As the day lengthens the cold strengthens' — an old gardeners' tale that is not far from the truth. The low late-winter sunlight and the noticeable lengthening of the days may hint that spring is not far away, but don't be deceived. February is the month most likely to have snow.

In many south-facing and sunny gardens the crocuses and some other bulbs will be showing colour. As you walk around the garden you will notice small changes in many plants; buds are beginning to get bigger and some are sticky.

Now is the time to plant any deciduous trees and shrubs. Try planting some early potatoes in a bucket or very large pot; if you keep them frost free, they should be ready to harvest in June. Inside you can grow the salad plant, cress, fresh food in the winter.

ACTIVITY SHEETS
*8. EXPERIMENTING WITH SOIL
*19. GROWING POTATOES IN A BUCKET
*26. WATCHING SEEDS GERMINATE

March

March

With some colourful flowers appearing, you may think that spring has arrived with the month of March, but the winter weather can linger. March can be windy and cold with clear, bright days and frosty nights. At the end of the month when the clocks go forward and we get lighter evenings, there is the distinct impression that spring is here and everything has started to grow.

Don't be too eager to start planting seeds into open ground, as generally the soil will be too wet and cold, and seeds, onion sets and potatoes will rot and die if planted too early. Early seed sowing should be into trays and pots that are protected by the warmth of a greenhouse or placed on a windowsill where the germinating plants will be protected from any March frost.

Over the coming spring months, it is a good idea to prepare vegetable and bedding plots for planting and hoe any seedling weeds. Repair the lawn; damaged and bare areas can be reseeded with new grass seed, purchased from a nursery or garden centre. A balanced fertiliser should be applied to the lawn in the spring when the weather is warm and plants are starting to grow.

As you walk around the garden you will notice that tree and shrub buds are swelling, many new young shoots are pushing through the soil and birds are busy building nests and singing their hearts out in the process.

ACTIVITY SHEETS
*9. MAKING A MINI COMPOST HEAP
13. SOWING SEEDS
21. WHAT ARE MY VEGETABLES WORTH?

Daffodils

Lesser spotted woodpecker

April

April showers can be heavy and come along unexpectedly between periods of warm sunshine; there may also be sleet, hail and thunder, but as the sun reappears, look out for a glorious rainbow that can accompany it. This is the type of spring weather to encourage plant growth; the days are getting longer and warmer and the garden has become a bustling, busy place.

Every day you will find that something needs to be done: preparing the ground for sowing or planting-out, weeding, potting-up, labelling and many other 'spring-cleaning' jobs. When you take a rest from all the garden tasks, spend a few quiet minutes looking and listening for birds and other wildlife that are also about their business at this busy time of the year; towards the end of the month you may hear the cuckoo.

If the weather is good, now is the time to sow vegetable seeds into open ground that is not wet and muddy; carrots, beetroot, peas, swede, cabbage and radishes are easy to grow and generally don't disappoint. It is still advisable to sow salad crops, lettuce and tomatoes into pots or trays and plant them outside later. The same applies to runner beans, sweetcorn, courgettes, onions, leeks and sunflowers. This gives them a good start before planting outside after all signs of frost have disappeared. Remember to protect any early crops from frost using a cloche or fleece.

ACTIVITY SHEETS
15. GROWING SUNFLOWERS
27. MAKING A FLORAL NECKLACE

Cuckoo

93

May

May is the month of blossoms, blooms and every shade of green as plants are growing rapidly. The new soft leaves on trees, shrubs and early flowering plants bring wonderful smells and colours to the garden for the first time in the new season's growth.

Particularly impressive are the spring flowering rhododendrons and azaleas that burst into magnificent flower, hiding their normal evergreen foliage for a few weeks at this time of the year. The magnolias, whose flowers appear before their leaves, and camellias, can be equally enthralling and will flower earlier than most rhododendrons. We are now entering a very busy gardening period with plenty to do. Plan your jobs well in advance and stick to your plan.

May is generally a gentle and reliable month regarding the weather, but if there are prolonged periods of rain don't let this interrupt a busy time. There will be many jobs you can do under cover in the garden shed or greenhouse, in particular the cleaning and tidying jobs that are important for plant health and help prevent pests and diseases, such as cleaning dirty pots and containers.

One little plant that is easy to grow and will give you masses of colorful flowers that smell wonderful is the sweet pea. Put a couple of seeds into a pot to get them growing and when the plants are 10–15 cm (4–6 in) high, carefully transfer the pot's contents to a large container or open soil; you will not be disappointed. Sweet peas like plenty of moisture and if you pick the flowers regularly they will keep going until the end of the summer.

As plants start to grow, particularly vegetables, they become a very tasty source of food for insects, slugs and snails. Make sure that these

Rhodedendron

creepy-crawlies do not eat your vegetables and fruit before you harvest them.

Vegetable plants such as onions, shallots, cabbage, potatoes, leeks, swede and parsnips can now be planted or pricked-out into open ground.

Top-dress the grass on your lawn with a general lawn fertilizer.

Don't try to work in the garden if it's too wet; you will make a horrible mess that can compact and damage the soil so that seedling plants find it difficult to grow. Frost can still occur at this time of year so listen to the weather forecast and remember to cover any tender plants.

ACTIVITY SHEETS
7. BUG SAFARI
14. PRICKING-OUT AND PLANTING-ON
28. KEEPING CUT FLOWERS FRESH

June

'Flaming June' is the right phrase for this time of the year as we are now into summer and the garden is a riot of colour, growth and activity. Some of the early flowering plants will be past their best while others will go on flowering for weeks to come, and some will not reach their peak until late summer. All this activity ensures a spectacular display. Now is the time to plant hanging baskets, window boxes and any other decorative containers.

Any vegetables that were planted in the spring will now be established and growing well, as will the constant problem for all gardeners — weeds! After all the weeding and tidying jobs are finished you can pick some nice, juicy, red strawberries and early raspberries that should be ready before the month is out.

Successive sowings of lettuce and radishes will ensure a continuous supply for summer salads. Runner beans can now be planted or pricked-out into open ground if they were sown into pots.

Try planting some herbs. Herbs make good little pot plants and are easy to grow. Parsley, sage, rosemary, thyme, dill, basil, mint and coriander will make a good, cheap display; they are nice to look at, have an attractive smell and can add a wonderful flavour when used for cooking and pickling.

Take some time to tidy up clumps of spring-bulb leaves; tie them back or, if they are turning brown, cut them off; slugs and snails love to get under these leaves and at night, in moist, weedy areas, they will pop out and eat any tasty vegetable and flower plants that are growing nearby.

Over the summer months, while you should cut the lawn regularly (always remembering that children should not use electrical garden equipment such as a lawnmower), never cut grass too short or the lawn will dry out and look terrible during dry periods. Grass cuttings make excellent compost. Early summer is a good time to kill lawn weeds, particularly perennials, when they are growing vigorously.

Remember to put tools away and leave the garden tidy. A garden can hide many hazards so always be alert to things that could cause injury, especially when you are using tools when other people may be nearby.

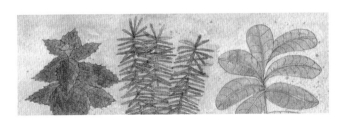

Remember, only adults should mow the lawn!

July

This is generally the driest time of the year. You will have to water some plants regularly or they will not produce their best results and could die. Hanging baskets, containers and seed trays will definitely require watering twice a day in very dry, hot weather. Don't over water and don't waste time and effort watering a lawn as this encourages shallow root growth. Only water garden plants that will benefit: vegetables and young flowering plants. Maintain watering until plants are established or the rain comes; occasional watering only encourages shallow rooting and your plants will suffer. Never saturate plants, particularly indoor pot plants; soil/compost should be damp not wet. If you can, stand your plant pots in a bowl of water for a few minutes; this gives them a good drink. And now is the time to put house plants outside for their summer holiday and a good breath of fresh air!

Butterflies and moths pollinate plants

The first vegetables should be ready to harvest in early July; salad lettuce, radishes, small beetroot and early potatoes and peas will bring fresh flavour from the garden to your plate. Wonderful!

We are now into holiday time when you may have to leave the garden to its own devices while you are away. Place your pots and containers in a shady spot out of direct sunlight and try to arrange for someone to water them regularly — a couple of times a week should be enough. Leave your garden as tidy as you can, because even in a week you will be astonished to find how quickly plants grow and get out of hand.

Make time to enjoy the garden. Sit quietly in a sunny corner and observe what is going on all around: bees and butterflies will be busy inspecting the plants that you have grown; it will give you a good feeling of achievement.

ACTIVITY SHEETS
*10. DRAWING AND NAMING PLANTS
20. GROWING PLANTS IN SHOPPING BAGS

August

The early part of August can be wet and unsettled. Thunder showers and longer periods of rain refresh the garden after the drier weather of June and July. To prolong the flowering life of plants, particularly roses, geraniums and those colourful flowers in hanging baskets, pick off any dead flowers (dead-heading); this practice encourages plants to go on developing more flowers rather than channeling all their energy into producing seeds once the flower has died. Tie back any straggling plants and keep weeding!

Some vegetables that were sown or planted-out in the spring will now be ready to harvest; potatoes, runner beans, peas, early carrots and beetroot as well as salad crops such as radish, lettuce and tomatoes will give you the taste of summer. Keep sowing a succession of salad crops; some salad crops and herbs can be sown and harvested quite quickly, in only six to eight weeks.

During any of the summer months, it is a good time to take shoot-tip cuttings of fuchsias, penstemons and geraniums. Root them around the edge of 10 cm (4 in) pots filled with sandy compost and place in a cool greenhouse or outside. Shade them from direct sunlight and keep the compost moist, not wet. You'll find that they will root easily and give you new plants to over-winter away from any frost.

If you want to do some fun growing make a 'grass head'. Grass grows at quite a speed and these 'grass heads' can be made at any time of the year: outside in the spring and summer, inside in the autumn and winter.

Grass heads

Dead-heading

September

As the holiday season draws to a close for another year and the last weeks of summer show the garden and flowering plants at their glorious best, we must think about the coming of autumn. Already the evenings are starting to draw in and they are noticeably cooler, although the days can still be sunny and hot with high temperatures.

September is the month of harvest festivals and garden shows; churches, village halls and meeting rooms will throng with the produce of local gardeners encouraged to show off the flowers, fruit and vegetables that can be grown in the garden or allotment. Chutney, pickles, jam and other delicious food can be preserved and used during the winter. Now is the time to go gathering the free fruits of the countryside; brambles (blackberries) are easy to find in hedgerows and they make delicious pie fillings and bramble jelly. Apples will also be ready for picking; watch out for wasps as they too like the taste of a ripe apple, particularly those on the ground.

Frost can occur early in September and put paid to some tender summer plants if they are not protected. In some years, the first frost can be late and the growing season is extended by an 'Indian summer', a term used by gardeners when good weather continues well into the autumn. Many birds that are summer visitors have already flown to their warmer winter homes, but there is still plenty of garden activity and things to do. Now is the time to plant potatoes into a bucket or container for a Christmas harvest.

Rake (scarify) the lawn as much as possible in autumn months to remove leaves, moss and other debris.

Any dead plants can be consigned to the compost heap and there will be bare patches in the vegetable plot after crops have been harvested. Now is the time to sow some over-wintering vegetables: spring cabbage, winter lettuce and early broad beans.

As plants die, collect some of their seeds in an envelope; make sure that the seed is dry and the name of the plant is written on the envelope. Next spring you will be able to sow these seeds and produce new plants; you could be surprised by the results.

ACTIVITY SHEETS
16. SEED COLLECTING
*31. DRYING FLOWERS AND LEAVES
*32 FLORAL DECORATIONS

A garden show

October

Autumn has now arrived, bringing with it the 'season of mists and mellow fruitfulness'. October is a month noted for garden colour: the red, brown, yellow and golden appearance of plants, particularly shrubs and trees, that indicates the end of summer and nature's preparation for winter.

The weather now becomes more unsettled and varies from still, damp, misty days to gales around the time of the equinox (equal length of daylight and darkness hours). The rain and wind will blow leaves from trees and generally give the garden an untidy appearance, with rubbish collecting in sheltered corners and on pathways. This is the time to sweep leaves and other garden rubbish into piles and put them on to the compost heap. Keep lawns and pathways swept and free of slippery leaves.

Although many of the vegetables that were sown in the spring will have been harvested, there will still be some root vegetables that should be lifted before the ground becomes too wet. Potatoes, carrots and beetroot can be stored in a cool, dark, dry place and used when needed. Try pickling cooked beetroot in vinegar. If your courgettes have grown to marrow size,

they will need to be harvested; soft vegetables will not stand any frost. Some vegetables such as winter cabbage, leeks and swede can be left in the ground longer as they can tolerate cold wet weather and frost. Winter and spring cabbage and leeks can be lifted from the garden plot when required throughout the winter.

Halloween is at the end of the month and if you want to have some fun, why not make a Halloween lantern. A marrow, pumpkin or swede can be hollowed out and made into a scary face.

ACTIVITY SHEETS
*23. FRESH FRUIT TASTING
*11. TREES

Pumpkin lantern

ovember

November

After the clocks have changed, the daylight hours shorten and cold, wet weather sets in. The garden can look drab and untidy; pull out all those annual bedding plants that have finished flowering and cut back other dead plants. Put them all on the compost heap along with the leaves that you have been sweeping from the lawn and pathways.

The contents of hanging baskets and containers that were planted for summer colour can also be dumped on the compost heap; now is the time to replant some of these containers and baskets with bulbs and winter flowers such as colourful pansies and primroses. These plants can keep flowering through to the spring; they will liven up any bare garden patches during the winter months before the first daffodils appear.

Leave leeks, swede, parsnips, cabbage and sprouts in the ground for over-wintering vegetables. Bring any tender plants inside.

November is traditionally the bonfire season, a good time to burn woody plants and other accumulated garden rubbish on bonfire night. It is also the time to start preparing ground for next year's planting. Digging is good exercise and will keep you warm. All the ground with nothing growing in it — bare flower beds and the vegetable plot — can be turned over and left to the action of the weather to break it down. Next spring the ground will be easy to work and form a seedbed.

Although nothing appears to be growing, the garden is still a fascinating place. Some winter flowers may appear on certain shrubs; the striking colours of various berries will attract birds, and the patterns that nature works on a frosty morning

Look out for garden visitors and encourage them with bird-feed

all bring interest and enjoyment. Look out for winter visitors, birds and animals.

As the leaves fall so do the fruits from nut trees; on a nice afternoon go hunting for nuts from chestnut and hazel trees and you may see some squirrels doing the same thing. You will also find the fruits of the horse chestnut tree: shiny brown conkers that have fallen out of their prickly outer shell. Try planting some in pots outside. The same can be done with the 'helicopter' seeds of the ash tree.

ACTIVITY SHEETS
18. GROWING SPRING BULBS IN POTS
*33. MAKING MONSTERS

December

December

Some gardeners consider December to be the end of the gardening year, while others think it's the beginning of the next, when plans and ideas are sorted out for another growing season. Get some plant and seed catalogues and start planning ahead for next year's gardening.

With festive activities and the unpleasant weather that is generally about at this time of the year, there is little chance to do much in the garden. Keep putting garden rubbish on to the compost heap and make sure that any plants that you hope to over-winter are protected from the frost: either well covered with straw and fleece or kept inside. Don't over water them!

Over the next few months when the weather is frosty, keep off the lawn or you will leave foot-marks. When the weather is dry and mild, give the grass a good rake (scarify) to remove moss and debris.

Get some help and try making a pot of garden vegetable soup using the vegetables you have grown. Very tasty!

Robin

Certain plants are associated with Christmas and can be used for decorations around the house; holly, ivy and other 'evergreens' are much in demand. Brighten up the home by making some simple Christmas decorations.

ACTIVITY SHEETS
*22. GARDEN VEGETABLE SOUP
34. CHRISTMAS DECORATIONS

Festive table decoration

Christmas wreath

Acknowledgments

As a youngster, my initial interest in gardening was fuelled by the regular source of pocket money obtained from my grandfather as I helped him maintain his garden. With patience and encouragement he stimulated my interest and I was slowly entrusted with the more exacting skills of growing flowers and vegetables in a small plot of my own. I did not enjoy the mundane tasks of weeding or sweeping pathways, but as we supped glasses of homemade ginger beer in the late evening sun and looked over a beautiful garden full of colour, fragrance and tasty vegetables, he would comment that this was the gardener's reward for all the effort; indeed a pleasant hobby and pastime that develops and remains with you for life. I am regularly reminded of this by my parents Dick and Olive Santer; both have green fingers!

With all the distractions of modern living, young people may not think of gardening as being an exciting, rewarding entertainment that can bring lifelong enjoyment and satisfaction. Many of the simple tasks and skills can be forgotten if you are not connected with and enthused by an experience that is dynamic and inexpensive.

In preparing this book I wanted young people to engage with gardening throughout the changing seasons of the year and I am indebted to a number of people who encouraged and assisted me in this quest.

In particular my colleagues at the Royal Caledonian Horticultural Society, Professor Fred Last, Tom Mabbott, Bruce Borrows, George Anderson, David Sinclair, RCHS council members over the past decade and the Suntrap Horticultural Centre; they have all been helpful beyond words with ideas and suggestions to make this publication appealing to young people.

Without colourful illustrations and photographs a book can prove most uninteresting to children. I am extremely grateful to Lucy McCririck for her imaginative and delightful illustrations; to Ian Gidney who, with the help of his colleagues at the West Lothian Camera Club, in particular William and Debra Mills and Stuart Robertson, have provided a number of wonderful photographs.

In their professional capacity, the publishers Floris Books have been exceptional with their guidance and assistance; Sally Martin, Catherine McKinney and Katy Lockwood-Holmes were always helpful and reassuring.

The success of a project such as this depends on family help: the support of Tessa, Ewan and, most importantly, my long-suffering wife Trish, without whose tolerance and skill in correcting my numerous mistakes, I would have foundered.